# If You Give a MouSe an iPhone

## Ann Droyd

**blue rider press**
A member of Penguin Group (USA)
New York

# For Kyra and Wyatt

With special thanks to Jeff Mack, David Hyde Costello, Diane deGroat, Shelley Rotner, Mordicai Gerstein, and Aaron Becker, who helped me through this and the forty-five drafts that preceded it.

blue
rider
press

Published by the Penguin Group
Penguin Group (USA) LLC
375 Hudson Street
New York, New York 10014

USA • Canada • UK • Ireland • Australia
New Zealand • India • South Africa • China

penguin.com
A Penguin Random House Company

ISBN 978-0-399-16926-7

Printed in the United States of America
10  9  8  7  6  5  4  3  2  1

Book design by David Milgrim

If you give a mouse an iPhone,

He's not going to ask for a cookie.
Or a glass of milk. Or anything at all.

In fact, he won't hear a word you say.

And if he doesn't hear a word you say, he won't know you are taking him on a special trip!

He'll miss out on all the kettle korn and funnel cake and ice cream and corn dogs and cheese fries and . . .

He won't even realize he's on the Katmandu Koaster.

TAP

TAP

Tap

Tap

And if he doesn't realize he's on the Katmandu Koaster, he won't remember to buckle his seat belt, and he'll probably take a little ride of his own.

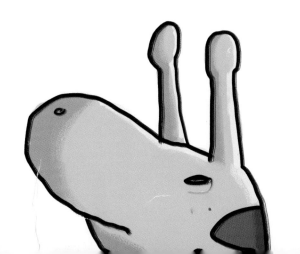

And chances are, if he takes
a little ride of his own,

# He'll accidentally open all the cages.

But he won't have the slightest
idea what's happening.

And if he doesn't know what's happening, he won't watch where he's going.

And he'll probably march right out
of the wild animal amusement park.

# And straight into the sea.

And if he falls into the sea . . .

So you'll have to get a boat. And you'll probably have to camp out for the night since it will be too late to paddle home.

Then, about the time you run out of energy, the phone battery will too.

And when the
battery runs out,

And when he totally freaks,
he'll probably beg you for a charger.

Please? Please?
Please?
PleasePlease Please?
Please?
Please?

And chances are, if he
begs you for a charger,

You'll point out that you are on a
remote island without any outlets . . .

And pretty soon
he'll forget all
about the charger.

And the iPhone to go with it.